ELMWOOD PARK PUBLIC LIBRARY
4 CONTI PARKWAY
ELMWOOD PARK, IL 60707
(708) 453-7645/8236

1. A fine is charged for each day a book is kept beyond the due date. The Library Board may take legal action if books are not returned within three months.

2. Books damaged beyond reasonable wear shall be paid for.

3. Each borrower is responsible for all books charged on this card and for all fines accruing on the same.

LOOKING INTO THE PAST:
PEOPLE, PLACES, AND CUSTOMS

Native American Talking Signs

by

Michael Kelly

Chelsea House Publishers

CHELSEA HOUSE PUBLISHERS

Editor-in-Chief Stephen Reginald
Managing Editor James D. Gallagher
Production Manager Pamela Loos
Art Director Sara Davis
Picture Editor Judy Hasday
Senior Production Editor Lisa Chippendale
Designers Takeshi Takahashi, Keith Trego

First Printing

1 3 5 7 9 8 6 4 2

Library of Congress Cataloging-in-Publication Data

Kelly, Michael.
North American Indian talking signs / by Michael Kelly.

   p. cm. — (Looking into the past)
Includes bibliographical references and index.
Summary: Directions for the signs for twenty-five words
used by various Native Americans accompanies information
about the customs, daily life, religious beliefs, and history of
these peoples.

ISBN 0-7910-4681-8 hc.
   1. Indian sign language—Juvenile literature. [1. Indian sign
language. 2. Indians of North America—Social life and customs.] I. Title. II. Series.
E98.S5K45 1997
419—dc21

97-26194
CIP
AC

CONTENTS

CULTURE, CUSTOMS, AND RITUALS

The important moments of our lives—from birth through puberty, aging, and death—are made more meaningful by culture, customs, and rituals. But what is culture? The word *culture,* broadly defined, includes the way of life of an entire society. This encompasses customs, rituals, codes of manners, dress, languages, norms of behavior, and systems of beliefs. Individuals are both acted on by and react to a culture—and so generate new cultural forms and customs.

What is custom? Custom refers to accepted social practices that separate one cultural group from another. Every culture contains basic customs, often known as rites of transition or passage. These rites, or ceremonies, occur at different stages of life, from birth to death, and are sometimes religious in nature. In all cultures of the world today, a new baby is greeted and welcomed into its family through ceremony. Some ceremonies, such as the bar mitzvah, a religious initiation for teenage Jewish boys, mark the transition from childhood to adulthood. Marriage also is usually celebrated by a ritual of some sort. Death is another rite of transition. All known cultures contain beliefs about life after death, and all observe funeral rites and mourning customs.

What is a ritual? What is a rite? These terms are used interchangeably to describe a ceremony associated with a custom. The English ritual of shaking hands in greeting, for example, has become part of that culture. The washing of one's hands could be considered a ritual which helps a person achieve an accepted level of cleanliness—a requirement of the cultural beliefs that person holds.

The books in this series, *Looking into the Past: People,*

Places, and Customs, explore many of the most interesting rituals of different cultures through time. For example, did you know that in the year A.D. 1075 William the Conqueror ordered that a "Couvre feu" bell be rung at sunset in each town and city of England, as a signal to put out all fires? Because homes were made of wood and had thatched roofs, the bell served as a precaution against house fires. Today, this custom is no longer observed as it was 900 years ago, but the modern word *curfew* derives from its practice.

Another ritual that dates from centuries long past is the Japanese Samurai Festival. This colorful celebration commemorates the feats of the ancient samurai warriors who ruled the country hundreds of years ago. Japanese citizens dress in costumes, and direct descendants of warriors wear samurai swords during the festival. The making of these swords actually is a separate religious rite in itself.

Different cultures develop different customs. For example, people of different nations have developed various interesting ways to greet each other. In China 100 years ago, the ordinary salutation was a ceremonious, but not deep, bow, with the greeting "Kin t'ien ni hao ma?" (Are you well today?). During the same era, citizens of the Indian Ocean island nation Ceylon (now called Sri Lanka) greeted each other by placing their palms together with the fingers extended. When greeting a person of higher social rank, the hands were held in front of the forehead and the head was inclined.

Some symbols and rituals rooted in ancient beliefs are common to several cultures. For example, in China, Japan, and many of the countries of the East, a tortoise is a symbol of protection from black magic, while fish have represented fertility, new life, and prosperity since the beginnings of human civilization. Other ancient fertility symbols have been incorporated into religions we still practice today, and so these ancient beliefs remain a part of our civilization. A more recent belief, the legend of Santa Claus, is the story of a kind benefactor who brings gifts to the good children of the world. This story appears in the lore of nearly every nation. Each country developed its own variation on the legend and each celebrates Santa's arrival in a different way.

New rituals are being created all the time. On April 21, 1997, for example, the cremated remains of 24 people were launched into orbit around Earth on a Pegasus rocket. Included among the group whose ashes now head toward their "final frontier" are Gene Roddenberry, creator of the television series *Star Trek,* and Timothy Leary, a countercultural icon of the 1960s. Each person's remains were placed in a separate aluminum capsule engraved with the person's name and a commemorative phrase. The remains will orbit the Earth every 90 minutes for two to ten years. When the rocket does re-enter Earth's atmosphere, it will burn up with a great burst of light. This first-time ritual could become an accepted rite of passage, a custom in our culture that would supplant the current ceremonies marking the transition between life and death.

Curiosity about different customs, rites, and rituals dates back to the mercantile Greeks of classical times. Herodotus (484–425 B.C.), known as the "Father of History," described Egyptian culture. The Roman historian Tacitus (A.D. 55–117) similarly wrote a lengthy account about the customs of the "modern" European barbarians. From the Greeks to Marco Polo, from Columbus to the Pacific voyages of Captain James Cook, cultural differences have fascinated the literate world. The books in the *Looking into the Past* series collect the most interesting customs from many cultures of the past and explain their origins, meanings, and relationship to the present day.

In the future, space travel may very well provide the impetus for new cultures, customs, and rituals, which will in turn enthrall and interest the peoples of future millennia.

Fred L. Israel
The City College of the City University of New York

CONTRIBUTORS

Senior Consulting Editor FRED L. ISRAEL is an award-winning historian. He received the Scribe's Award from the American Bar Association for his work on the Chelsea House series *The Justices of the United States Supreme Court.* A specialist in early American history, he was general editor for Chelsea's *1897 Sears Roebuck Catalog.* Dr. Israel has also worked in association with Dr. Arthur M. Schlesinger, jr. on many projects, including *The History of U.S. Presidential Elections* and *The History of U.S. Political Parties.* They are currently working together on the Chelsea House series *The World 100 Years Ago,* which looks at the traditions, customs, and cultures of many nations at the turn of the century.

Michael Kelly Ph.D., is a historian who has taught at the City College of New York and the State University of New York at Stony Brook. A former recipient of the Excellence Award at CCNY, which is awarded to the top graduate student, Michael has received research grants from the Truman Presidential Library and the Eisenhower Presidential Library. He is the author of numerous articles on American politics, including "The 1920 Presidential Election," and he currently is writing biographies of President Bill Clinton and U.S. Senator Jacob K. Javits.

OVERVIEW

The First Americans

Although spread out across an entire continent, the Indians of North America are all descended from the brave people who crossed the Bering Strait thousands of years ago. Those travelers and their descendants lived a nomadic existence, hunting for their food and warring with other tribes, and their signs reflect that lifestyle.

Although there were over 100 distinct Native American tribes living in North America between 1600 and 1900, most of them did not speak the same language. When two Indians from different tribes met in the vast forest of the northeast, the ice fields of the cold north, or the prairies of the far west, they communicated through simple hand signals and pantomime. Most North American Indians shared the same cultural heritage, so communicating basic concepts was quite simple.

This book describes 25 of the hand signals used by the Native Americans to communicate with one another and with the early explorers, traders, and colonists from Europe. The signs also give a reader insight into the simple life that the Native Americans lived. Although some tribes did have a written language, most chronicled the history of their people by drawing pictures on bear skins, buffalo robes, and deer hides.

This book also illustrates some of the customs, camp life, religious beliefs, and history of the original natives of North

America. As more Europeans settled on Indian land, the natives were continually pressed westward and eventually were moved to government reservations. By the beginning of the 20th century, almost all the Native Americans in the United States had been relegated to a life of poverty in a land that had once been theirs.

CHALLENGE

hen encountering a stranger at a distance in his own territory, an Indian would usually make the challenge for "Who goes there?" This challenge was made by raising the right hand and waving it back and forth. If the stranger was not an enemy he replied "friend" by clasping his hands together in front of his stomach. By clasping his hands in front of him, a stranger indicated that he meant no harm and was not holding a weapon in his hands. Tribes also challenged neighboring Native Americans by sending the chief a deer hide with a message of war, in many cases listing past grievances and the terms for peace if war was to be avoided.

In the woodlands of the northeast where many Native Americans traveled in small parties, chance encounters with warriors from other tribes, or European hunters, traders, and settlers were a common occurrence. When encountering other Indians, a warrior could sometimes recognize the

stranger's tribe, place in his people's hierarchy, prowess as a hunter or warrior, and other cultural signs that they shared in common. The same was not true for European encounters.

The only Indians who did not challenge strangers were the Eskimo, or Inuit, tribes of the Arctic. Because the region was so inhospitable, there were no large European settlements. The result was an area populated by one people who welcomed all strangers into their homes.

THE SEA

his sign was used chiefly by the tribes living on the Atlantic and Pacific coasts of North America and by the Inuit (Eskimo) living in the northern regions of Canada and the Arctic Circle. It was used to describe any large body of water, such as the Great Lakes or the Mississippi River. Most east coast tribes seldom ventured far from the coastline, but many of the Indians in the Great Northwest often ventured far out to sea in search of fish.

The Yurok, Chinook, and other tribes in the northwestern United States and southwestern Canada used their dugout canoes to roam along the shores of the Pacific Ocean. They hunted seals, sea lions, and other sea mammals off the coast of California. During the summer months, the Indians caught enough salmon to feed themselves throughout the winter months. Those fish that were not immediately eaten were dried on racks, salted, and stored in baskets or

underground pits away from marauding bears.

The Mimac Tribe of Nova Scotia fished in teams of canoes. The fishermen used nets to catch large quantities of cod and salmon. On occasion the Mimac ventured far off shore to capture porpoises, sea lions, and seals. When a whale was washed ashore, the entire tribe encamped on the beach and stripped the sea mammal of all its meat, blubber, bones, and teeth. With the coming of the white man, whale oil was traded for guns, iron kettles, and other items.

The sign is made by drawing the right hand in a wavy motion across the chest.

KNIFE

efore coming into contact with whites, Indian knives were usually made from antlers, animal bones (usually the ribs), bear claws, sharpened stones such as flint, hard woods, or seashells.

The knife was one of the most important tools in a warrior's arsenal. He used it in almost every aspect of his daily life. A warrior could use his knife to clean fish, skin animals, strip saplings, cut snares for traps, and perform a myriad of other chores.

In battle the knife was usually used for close combat when a rifle or bow and arrow would not suffice. After killing their enemies, some warriors used their knives to take the scalps of their fallen foes as war trophies.

In the 16th century, as more Europeans plied their trade among native peoples, metal knives began to replace the traditional Indian weapon. They were eagerly sought by all the tribes of North America, who traded beaver, deer, bear, elk,

moose, and buffalo pelts for the instruments. Metal knives could withstand extreme conditions and still maintain their sharp edge. Within a generation, the European knife had become a standard weapon of an Indian warrior, together with gun powder, a bag of bullets, and a flintlock rifle.

To make the sign for a knife, place the hands as shown and make a cutting motion with the right forefinger several times towards the tips of the left hand.

DEER

ost North American Indians hunted a form of deer. In the ice-covered north, near the Arctic Circle, the Eskimo followed the caribou herds, much like the Plains Indians followed the buffalo. A mature caribou weighed as much as 600 pounds, and its meat provided the Eskimos with a natural source of protein. The pelts were scraped and softened, and provided warm, lightweight clothing and covers for summer tepees. The animal's sinews were used to make thread, which was then used on moccasins, leggings, and winter garments. No part of the animal was wasted; caribou bones were used to make fish hooks, arrow heads, sewing needles, and knives, and the fat of the caribou was boiled down to make oil for campfires and lamps.

Another species of deer is the American elk, which roamed throughout much of the continental United States and was hunted by all tribes. A male elk could weigh as

much as 1,000 pounds and could feed a small village for weeks. Elk hides were prized for their softness and light weight. As with the buffalo, women of the tribe boiled the fat of the animal to make butter, and elk oil was rubbed on the body to repel insects. The antlers were used to make knives and stakes. The skin was dried on racks, softened, and sewn together to make pants, shirts, leggings, rope, and tepee covers. The soft underbelly of the animal was cut into strips and sewn together with rawhide thread to make waterproof moccasins.

The sign for deer indicated its horns, as shown. The back of the hands must face outward to avoid confusion with the sign for the buffalo.

PEACE

hen the leader of a tribe agreed to a peace treaty with another tribe or with the representatives of European or American governments, he usually kept his word. The same could not always be said for the British, French, or American peoples. The history of Native American peace treaties with European settlers is one of betrayal and lies.

In 1783, at the signing of the Treaty of Paris, the British ceded all lands east of the Mississippi River to the new American nation—despite the fact that both governments had previously signed land agreements with the tribes of the Iroquois Federation in order to win them as allies during the American Revolution. Many of the tribes which had fought side by side with the colonial army found that the American victory meant a loss of their ancestral homelands.

Peace treaties between Indian tribes in North America were common and far more lasting than those made with

Europeans. In the late 17th century, the Iroquois established a federation and made war on any tribe that disputed their authority to control the beaver pelt trade with the European traders. Their territory encompassed much of the northeast, stretching from the Canadian borders of New York State through much of the Great Lakes Region. The tribes that joined the Iroquois League prospered, and the peace between the tribes within the League lasted for decades.

The sign is made by raising the arms as shown while advancing slowly.

BEAR

ears used to be plentiful throughout much of North America. Brown and black bears roamed the northeastern woods, while the grizzly, which could reach a height of seven feet and weigh over 1,000 pounds, ranged west of the Mississippi and in the northwest. In the Arctic North lived the polar bear.

Before the introduction of the flintlock rifle to the tribes of North America, hunting bears was extremely dangerous and many warriors were clawed to death in their brave attempts. With a large head filled with razor-sharp teeth, and jaws strong enough to bite through a warrior's arm or leg, the bear was the most dangerous animal in the forests of North America. Most bears lived on a diet of nuts, honey, ants, wasps, plants, and other insects, and were shy and peaceful unless cornered. The Kodiak bear of Alaska lived almost entirely on salmon and green plants found in the area.

The Huron and Mohawk tribes raised some bears in captivity and butchered them for special ceremonial occasions. Bear claws were made into necklaces and were a symbol of potency, prowess, and bravery. Bear butter was considered a delicacy and was made from boiled bear fat.

Many of the Indians of the Great Plains considered bears sacred and tried to avoid killing them unless the tribe needed the meat to survive. In the woods, bear tracks looked much like those of a man, and many Indians believed the bear was infused with the spirit of dead warriors or fallen chieftains.

The sign is made by holding the fingers as shown, then making a clawing motion with the hand.

EAGLE

agles are birds of prey with strong bills, powerful toes, and razor-sharp claws. The eagle played an important role in Native American culture. Most tribes regarded the bird as sacred and a symbol of bravery. Eagle feathers were used on the headdresses and ornaments of chieftains to distinguish them from other warriors. Warriors were often granted eagle feathers by a chief for a particularly brave accomplishment in battle. Many tribes kept eagles in captivity in order to have easier access to their feathers. Some young warriors went on quests to seek the high perches of the eagle to acquire the feathers. To have an "eagle eye" was to have the ability to observe life with an exceptional keenness.

The Dakota Sioux of the Great Plains carved the symbol of the eagle on the top of their totem poles. The symbol represented both the ancestral past and the fruitful continuation of the tribe. Sitting Bull, the great war chief of the

Sioux, was said to have visions or dreams in which he flew high over the Plains seeking out the dangers posed to his people by the United States Calvalry and other Indian tribes.

When the representatives of the 13 colonies were searching for a symbol to represent their new nation, they chose the American bald eagle. They also placed eagles prominently on early peace treaties with various Indian nations.

The sign is made by placing the hands as shown and then sliding the right hand down over the left.

BATTLE

any of the Indian tribes of North America built their culture around the pursuit of war. By the early 17th century, the Iroquois League had consolidated its control over the lucrative beaver pelt trade by driving out or annihilating any tribe that stood in its way.

Native Americans also fought the European colonists' attempts to steal their land. In King Philip's War (1675–1677) the leader of the Wampanoags united the tribes of New England in an attempt to drive out the Puritans. However, the Native Americans were defeated and soon put on reservations. During the Seminole Wars in Florida and Georgia, the Seminoles were able to fend off white attempts to seize their land for more than two decades. Finally, in 1838, thousands of federal troops and state militia forced those members of the tribe that had not escaped to the Everglades to move to the "Indian Territories" west of the Mississippi River.

In one of the last battles on the Great Plains, the Sioux war chief Sitting Bull defeated the U.S. Seventh Cavalry, commanded by General George Custer, at the Battle of the Little Bighorn in 1876. However, by the 1890s most of the tribes of the Great Plains had been forced off their land and onto government reservations.

The sign is made by placing the arms as shown and moving the clenched fists backwards and forwards alternately. The sign is used to describe a battle which has taken place or to assert that a warrior "will do battle."

DWELLING

ll the tribes of North America adapted their lodgings to the natural environment. In the extreme north near the Arctic Circle, the Aleut and Eskimo built their igloos out of blocks of ice shaped in the form of a dome in order to withstand the strong winds and extreme cold. In the northeast, where there were many forests, Native Americans built their shelters from wood. The Penobscot tribe of Maine and Canada construct-ed small hemispheric cabins shingled with pieces of bark, and two doors, usually covered with deer or moose skin, were arranged to let in fresh air and allow smoke to escape.

The Iroquois Confederation, made up of the Seneca, Mohawk, Tuscarora, Oneida, Cayuga, and Onondaga tribes, inhabited much of the Great Lakes region. The tribes lived together in large communal wooden "longhouses," which could sometimes house as many as 100 families. The Fox and Winnebago tribes lived in small wigwams consisting of

an arched framework of saplings covered with animal hides, rush mats, and in some cases soft bark.

The Apache and Mescalaro tribes of the west and southwest built their small oval-shaped wickiups from grass, brushwood, and reed mats. The Pueblos built their dwellings with scooped-out floors to keep cool. The walls were a mixture of wood and mud mortar, and each home had a brush-covered roof supported by sturdy poles.

The nomadic Plains Indians usually covered their tepees with buffalo hides supported with long poles. These also served as a travois when the camp relocated.

The sign is made by placing the hands as shown in the form of a hut.

BUFFALO

illions of buffalo and bison roamed the plains of the United States in large herds, and the shaggy animals were a mainstay of the tribes of the Great Plains and central prairies. The Cheyenne, Kiowa, Shoshone, Crow, Blackfoot, Arapaho, and Sioux shared some of the same hunting grounds and built much of their culture around the buffalo.

The buffalo hunt was a communal effort, with the entire village participating. The very existence of many tribes often depended upon the success of this annual pursuit. The strategy was to kill as many animals as quickly as possible. Before horses became plentiful, the women of the tribe drove the buffalo within range of the waiting male hunters, who killed the animals with arrows and spears. As tribes gained more mobility by using horses, they were better able to pursue and kill stampeding herds.

After a buffalo was killed by the warriors, the women of

the tribe skinned the animal, pegged the hide tightly to the ground or on a wooden rack, and scraped it clean of fat and hair. The buffalo pelt was then made into a winter robe, or several were stitched together to make conical tepee covers.

No part of the buffalo was wasted. The tongue, considered a delicacy, was eaten first. Bone marrow was boiled down to make butter, and any meat that was not eaten immediately was dried and preserved for the winter encampment, when game was scarce.

The sign is made as shown. It should not be confused with the sign for deer.

WEAPON

Before they came into contact with Europeans, the weapon used by most Native Americans in hunting and battle was the bow and arrow. In the northeast most bows were made from yew, hickory, or ash wood and were about four feet long. The Plains Indians used willow and aspen for their bows. Arrowheads were shaped from deer antler, eagle claws, flint, hard stone, or wood, and sharpened to a razor's edge. The arrows were made from various reeds and wood, and were fitted at the end with feathers to help the arrow maintain a straight line in flight. Because of the poor accuracy of their bows, most hunters shot their prey from close range.

Another weapon favored by Indians was the tomahawk, an Algonquin term for club. Before the coming of the Europeans, these weapons were usually wooden ball-headed clubs, in many cases spiked with sharpened stones, animal claws, bird beaks, or seashells. In the mid-17th century these

wooden tools were replaced with metal hatchets obtained from European traders in exchange for animal skins and beaver pelts. The tribes of the Iroquois Confederation and the Great Plains used the tomahawk in their religious ceremonies by smoking tobacco in the small pipe bowl located next to the blade.

As trade grew between settlers and Native Americans, many Indians gained access to guns and became proficient in their use. A rifle, powder horn, and bullet bag quickly became standard equipment for most warriors.

The sign is made by going through the motions of drawing a bow and shooting an arrow.

CANOE OR BOAT

orth American Indians were skillful at adapting to their natural environment, and they learned from an early age how to utilize to their best advantage the vast network of rivers, lakes, and streams that surrounded them. The favorite mode of river travel was by canoe. Made as light as possible, usually from birch bark, the canoe was narrow in the middle and closed at both ends; averaging ten feet long, it was able to carry an entire household or, in times of war, a small war party. Before the Indians acquired horses, the canoe was used for travel to trap and trade, or to move from summer to winter encampments.

Another river craft favored by the Indians was the dugout canoe. It was usually made of a pine, oak, or cedar log, which was hollowed out by burning and scraping. A typical dugout canoe could carry as many as 40 warriors, and some of the canoes were as long as 50 feet. The Ottawa

tribe added sails to many of their larger canoes and plied their trade on Lake Michigan.

In the Arctic, Eskimos constructed a different type of water craft which they called a kayak. Because of the severe weather conditions, the kayak was made with a frame covered with seal skins with only a small opening cut in the middle of the craft. Unlike the traditional Indian canoe, the kayak was propelled by one double-bladed paddle. A few of the tribes in the northwest and Canada also built sturdy rowing boats with which they pursued the salmon that spawned in the rivers and creeks of the area.

The sign is made by adopting the posture and movements of a man paddling a canoe.

BRAVERY

The culture of the Native Americans of North America was based on a warrior society, and bravery in battle was considered a positive quality. The Apache, Mescalaro, and Chiricahua of the Southwest prided themselves on raiding the livestock of other tribes as well as that of white settlements in Arizona and New Mexico. One of the highest forms of bravery was "counting coup," wherein a warrior touched a live adversary with a spear or took a piece of clothing as a trophy.

A warrior's courage was often judged by his war trophies. The Mohawks and Hurons would often return to camp with the scalps of their enemies, which they would display as proof of their prowess at war. The Iroquois placed bravery among their highest honors, and when a prisoner captured in battle stood up well to their torture he was sometimes eaten by his captors in tribute to his courage.

Many captured warriors sang a death song in defiance as they were slowly burned at the stake and eaten.

Another form of bravery among many of the tribes of North America was the vision quest. Soon after reaching puberty, a boy would leave the village alone to seek a vision. During his stay in the wild he fasted and prayed to the Great Spirit for guidance. His visions took the form of dreams, and when the boy returned to his people it was with the knowledge that he had a guardian spirit to help guide him through life.

The sign is made with both hands, as shown.

THE GREAT SPIRIT

ost North American Indians shared a common belief in a higher being and the continuation of the spirit after death. Throughout the continent, tribes practiced many ceremonies and rituals to ward off evil, bring about a good hunt or harvest, celebrate a victory, or mourn a death.

Many Native Americans carried personal amulets or tokens to ensure good luck and ward off evil spirits. Indeed, all Indians shared the same belief in personal visions and guardian spirits. They were guided in their belief by the tribe's shaman, or medicine man, who interpreted dreams, healed body and soul, and communicated with the spirit world on their behalf.

The North American Indian peoples varied in the way they worshipped. For the Sioux, Cheyenne, Arapaho, and other tribes of the Great Plains, one of the most sacred ceremonies of the year was the Sun Dance, where the entire

tribe fasted, danced, and prayed for four days and nights to renew its bond with the Great Spirit.

In the Arctic, the Eskimo were also guided by their shamans. The holy men of the tribe could aid hunters in locating seals and sea lions, cure diseases, help control the weather, and pave the way to the spirit world for the dead.

In the woodlands of the northeast many tribes celebrated the annual Green Corn Ceremony, which lasted for four days. The people of the tribe fasted, burned their old clothing, and finally feasted on corn and venison in celebration of a good harvest.

The sign is made by extending the arms and hands as shown.

EATING

ative Americans' diets varied according to the region where their tribe dwelled. The nomadic Eskimo of the Arctic were forced to follow game the entire year and existed almost entirely on seal, fish, polar bear, walrus, sea lion, caribou, and if they were lucky, white whale.

The Chocktaw, Shawnee, Fox, and Sauk tribes of the northeastern woodlands were surrounded by an abundance of natural riches. In addition to hunting black bear, mountain lion, cougar, and possum, they regularly feasted on turkey, pheasant, duck, and goose. Many of the tribes of the Iroquois Confederation planted large fields of corn, which was harvested and stored in drums or in underground bins to feed the tribe in the winter months.

The Sioux, Cheyenne, Blackfoot, and other tribes of the Great Plains had an abundant source of game. Among their mainstays were the grizzly bear, mountain lion, deer, elk, and

moose. Most important, however, was the buffalo. By the 1870s white hunters had invaded the Indian hunting grounds in large numbers, and within a decade they had killed more than 10 million buffalo. They took the animal's hide, leaving the rest of the carcass to rot in the sun. By the 1880s the buffalo was almost extinct and white farmers were selling their bones for $5 per ton. The bones were then made into fertilizer.

The sign is made by putting the right hand before the mouth as shown and moving it in a small circle three times.

PARENTS

he tribe was an extended family for all children, who were recognized as the future of the tribe and cared for by all. Young boys and girls were taught at an early age how to contribute to the well-being of their tribe. Native American parents raised their sons to be independent, brave, and good hunters. Boys benefited from the closeness of extended families; uncles were like second fathers and often treated their nephews as one of their own sons. If parents were lost in battle, relatives adopted the orphans.

In many tribes, parents usually arranged the marriage of their daughters to a good provider and hunter, in exchange for a dowry of gifts or horses. On the Great Plains among the Sioux, a mother moved in with her daughter's family if her own husband was killed in battle.

The tribes of the Iroquois Confederation developed the practice of replacing dead children or relatives by abducting

captives from other tribes and bestowing on them the life of the deceased. If a kidnapped child was replacing the son of a chief, he was automatically given the respect, possessions, and stature of the chief's child.

For most Native Americans, the right hand, arm, or side indicated men and the left hand, arm, or side indicated women. The sign to indicate parents is made by closing the fist and touching the right breast for father or the left breast for mother.

LEAVING

Many of the tribes of the Great Plains, such as the Sioux, Cheyenne, and Blackfeet, lived a nomadic existence. The tribes followed the herds of buffalo on their seasonal migrations.

When the decision was made to break camp, the Native Americans wrapped their possessions and provisions and tied them to tent poles, which were dragged by horses or dogs. The sick, elderly, and very young were pulled along behind the horses on a travois, which was a buffalo robe tied between tent poles.

Before the arrival of white settlers, the tribes of the Great Plains could move across the vast landscape unhindered, but as more white settlers moved onto Indian land the seasonal migrations became more difficult. Many tribes had traditionally summered and wintered in specific areas for hundreds of years. After the American Civil War, the Great Plains witnessed an influx of white settlers who chose to

ignore Indian land customs. Whites viewed land as empty or deserted if there was no dwelling or permanent occupant. When the tribes returned from their winter camps they often found their ancestral camp had been settled and fenced in by white interlopers.

The most brutal relocation of Indians occurred in the 1830s when all the people of the Cherokee Nation were removed from their ancestral homes in the Carolinas and Georgia and forced to march 2,000 miles to a new home in the Oklahoma Territory under the guns of the United States Army. The Cherokee dubbed the forced trek the "Trail of Tears," and thousands died from lack of food and proper clothing during the march.

The sign is made by placing the hands as shown, then dropping the upper hand over the lower.

I AGREE

n general, North American Indians could be trusted to keep their promises and obligations unless they believed they were being deceived. Unfortunately, in their dealings with white men, and particularly with the United States government after the American Revolution, Native Americans were often cheated out of their ancestral land.

After the 13 colonies won their independence from Great Britain, the colonial government assumed jurisdiction over Native American affairs. In the early years of the United States, the government recognized many Indian tribes as independent nations and concluded treaties with chieftains who ceded their land for monetary compensation. However, problems arose when tribes which had not agreed to the treaties refused to give up their territories. These tribes usually were forced off the land without compensation.

In 1838, the enactment of the Indian Removal Act by

Congress led to one of the worst examples of Native American resettlement. Under the Indian Removal Act, the U.S. sought title to all the ancestral land of the Cherokee Nation in the Appalachian Mountains of North Carolina. Although the leaders of the tribe succeeded in convincing the United States Supreme Court to declare the act unconstitutional, President Andrew Jackson nevertheless ordered the army to forcefully remove the Indians. In the resulting 2,000-mile forced march to the Oklahoma Territory, 4,000 Cherokees died from malnutrition, disease, and frostbite.

To make the sign for agree, first place the hand as shown, then close the fist and lower it to the chest while bowing the head slowly.

TREES

rees played an integral part in the daily life of many North American Indians. They provided the people with fuel, tools, implements, and weapons. The bark of some trees was used for medicinal purposes, and other trees were regarded as sacred.

The Indian tribes of the eastern woodlands, which included the Seneca, Mohawk, Tuscarora, Oneida, Cayuga, and Onondaga tribes, lived among vast forests of ash, birch, elm, pine, hemlock, hickory, oak, fir spruce, and poplar. These tribes favored the wood of the hickory and ash trees for their bows. For their war clubs they used the hard wood of the oak tree. The light bark of the birch tree provided material for canoes.

The Iroquois venerated both the elm and the white pine. They used basswood bark and elm to make rope, and used many of the herbaceous plants found in the forest for medicine. They tapped the sugar maple tree for its sweet sap,

made oil from hickory trees, and collected acorns and chest-
nuts to adorn their dinner tables and eat during winter.

In the northwestern United States, the Chinook and
Yurok tribes carved totemic symbols on a sacred pole. These
symbols traced family lineage and the history of the tribe,
and praised the spirits. They called these carved pillars
totem poles.

On the Great Plains, the Sioux and Cheyenne used wood
from the aspen and willow tree for their bow and arrows.

To make the sign for a single tree place the hands and
fingers as shown. More than one tree is indicated by
extending two or more fingers of the right hand.

HORSE

ative Americans first came into contact with horses in the mid-to-late 16th century. An explorer, Francisco Vásquez de Coronado, brought Spanish thoroughbreds with him from Spain and lost many of them during his expedition through Mexico and the Rio Grande. Coranado and his men were probably the first whites ever seen by the Pueblo, Hopi, Tewa, Pecos, and Apache tribes.

The Plains Indians also came into contact with horses in the late 16th century. They attained many of their horses through trade with settlers or by hunting and taming the wild herds that roamed the Plains. By the 1750s horses played an important part in all aspects of tribal life. When traveling to or from a hunt, the Shawnee, Dakota, Sioux, Blackfeet, and other tribes built travois consisting of two tepee poles with a platform in the middle attached with rawhide rope. A family's possessions were placed on the

device, which was then fastened over a horse's shoulder and dragged behind it. Before they acquired horses Indians had attached their travois to dogs.

The horse allowed the Plains Indians to travel greater distances in shorter periods, pursue the buffalo herds, and make war on neighboring tribes. The acquisition and retention of large herds of horses soon became paramount to the success of a tribe. In gaining horses for the tribe, young warriors could attain status among their peers. When proposing marriage, a gift of a string of horses to the parents of the bride was quite common.

In making the sign the lower hand indicates the horse, and the upper hand is rocked to and fro to indicate the rider.

THE WHITE MAN

hen the white man first arrived in North America, Indians occupied the entire continent. The Native Americans had over 2,000 separate dialects, and an estimate of the native population when Columbus arrived in the Americas in 1492 is 50 million.

The early explorers, traders, and colonists came chiefly from Spain, Portugal, Holland, France, and England, and were referred to as "palefaces" by the Indians they encountered. In the 16th century the Spanish conquistadors set out to find gold in the New World and conquered and enslaved many of the native peoples they met.

French traders and explorers established trading posts among many of the tribes of the Great Lakes region and the Northeast. Before the American Revolution, the Iroquois and other tribes aligned themselves with the French and battled the encroachment of the British settlers in New Eng-

land and elsewhere. The French were more interested in trade and military alliances than settlement, and many Indian leaders considered them natural allies.

The British government also courted the allegiance of the Indian tribes in its effort to keep American colonists in check. During the American Revolution many of the tribes allied themselves with the British Empire and were treated as defeated enemies when the Americans attained their independence and ratified the Treaty of Paris in 1783.

The sign is made by drawing the forefinger across the forehead from left to right.

HIDE OR
TAKE COVER

he natives of North America were skillful hunters and exercised great cunning and patience in stalking wild game. They had to, because the survival of the tribe often depended on their success. Because they lived so close to nature, many Indians knew the habits and hiding places of the animals they sought.

During the buffalo hunt, warriors would camouflage their scent by rubbing buffalo fat all over their bodies. When they approached the buffalo herd, it was always from downwind, and, covered with heavy buffalo robes, they slowly crawled up to their prey.

The Indians of North America were at home in the forest, and could easily hide in case of danger. In addition, if Native Americans found themselves trapped in a sudden storm, they knew where to take cover. Most Indians traveled light and relied on their knowledge of their surroundings

for shelter and food.

Indians used the same tactics when they were fighting a war with other tribes or with Europeans. Their stealth made them particularly effective against the European military tactic of standing out in the open and firing volleys of bullets at adversaries.

During the French and Indian Wars (1754–1763), the French government enlisted Indian aid in their war against the English. The Huron and Mohawk tribes wreaked havoc throughout New England through the use of cleverly devised ambushes. The settlers of New England protected themselves by adopting Indian tactics.

The sign is made by extending the left hand as shown and placing the right hand over the left. This sign also means to hide something, someone, or oneself.

DANGER

his was one of the most common signs used by North American Indians. They faced constant danger in their everyday life, either from neighboring tribes, wild animals, the elements, or European settlers.

Even in the best of times, Indians confronted hazards all around them. The Sioux, Cheyenne, Blackfeet, and other tribes of the Great Plains, although sometimes surrounded by millions of buffalo, faced the constant danger of starvation. Before horses were introduced, the tribe depended almost solely on the traditional migration pattern of the buffalo. If for some reason the bison changed their route, the Indians would not have enough food for the winter. Even if they were fortunate enough to find the herds, they faced the possibility of death or capture by another tribe's hunting parties.

Disease was a constant threat to every Indian tribe.

There were no antibiotics to arrest infection, and death from simple wounds was commonplace. Also, when the Europeans first came into contact with Indians, they brought more than trade goods. Diseases such as smallpox and chicken pox wiped out millions of Native Americans who had not developed an immunity to these new forms of death from Europe.

The Indians also had to face the vagaries of the elements. In severe winters, game was scarce, and the weaker members of the tribe perished. If the summer was too dry, the tribes faced drought and starvation.

This sign is made as shown, with the hand pointed in the direction in which the danger lies. It can be followed by some other sign to indicate the origin of the danger.

HONESTY

he Native Americans of North America lived a rugged but simple life. Honor and bravery were prized above all else. When a warrior gave his word to another it was with the understanding that both parties would keep their bargain. Most Indian tribes had no written language and paid little attention to written documents. This was a satisfactory way of life as long as there were only Indians dwelling on the continent. But once the Europeans arrived in large numbers, this simple method of keeping agreements and bargains was no longer enough.

Many white men who first encountered Native Americans sought the leader of their tribe. In many cases, after presenting gifts or making trades, the chief would be asked to "make his mark" upon a parchment. Most chiefs could assure their guests that they and their people would honor the agreement. Problems arose when white settlers sought

to make these temporary trade or land use agreements permanent.

Even when Indian tribes made a binding agreement and lived by its terms, they were usually cheated. In 1791 the United States recognized the Cherokee territory in Georgia as an independent nation. But in 1838, in defiance of the Supreme Court, President Andrew Jackson illegally forced the Cherokee off their ancestral land.

Used by itself, this sign indicated good faith and honesty.

GOOD OR GENUINE

hen Native Americans gave their pledge to another Indian or later to Europeans and Americans, they could be trusted to keep their bargains.

During the American Revolution, the colonists appealed to the Indian tribes for help in their battle against the British Empire. The most powerful Indian federation during this period was the Iroquois League. The American patriots invoked freedom when they made their case before the leaders of the league, convincing many of the Indian leaders that Great Britain also posed a threat to their future freedom. Many of the Indians identified with the colonists' cause and fought side by side with them throughout the eight-year conflict. Other tribes fought with the British.

However, at the closing of hostilities all Indians faced the same peril—the loss of their ancestral land. Unfortunately, the Americans, after throwing off the yoke of British Imperi-

alism, were not willing to continue to view the Indian as an ally. In their peace agreement with Great Britain, the new American government demanded and recieved illegal title to all Indian lands east of the Mississippi River. This would be only the first land grab by the new American nation. For the next 100 years, Indian tribes throughout the continent would sign treaties they believed to be good and genuine, only to realize later that they had been deceived.

To signal good or genuine you place the right hand palm downwards over the heart and then draw the right hand across the heart.

CHRONOLOGY

7,000–4,000 B.C. – nomadic tribes from Asia cross a land bridge at the Bering Strait onto the North American continent.

4,000 B.C.–A.D.1492 – Separate tribes of Native Americans grow and flourish in North America. By the time of Columbus's arrival, there were an estimated 50 million Native Americans in the New World.

1620 – The Pilgrims land at Plymouth Rock, founding one of the earliest European settlements in the New World. The Pilgrims were assisted by Native American tribes living nearby.

1689–1748 – Native Americans fight a series of wars against British colonists, assisted by the French. These included King William's War (1689-1697), Queen Anne's War (1702-1713), and King George's War (1744-1748).

1754–1763 – The French and Indian Wars, or the Seven Years War, ends in victory for the British, who take control of Canada and western North America. In 1763, Chief Pontiac of the Ottowa Tribe leads an uprising against the British, which fails.

1775–1783 – The American Revolution pits Great Britain against its colonists in the new world. Native Americans fight with both the colonists and British.

1811 – Tecumseh, an Native American chief, leads an uprising, but is defeated at the Battle of Tippecanoe. Tecumseh later fights with the British during the War of 1812.

1838 – The Cherokee nation is forced off its land, taking the 2,000-mile "Trail of Tears" to Oklahoma.

1867 – Sioux Chief Red Cloud leads opposition to settlers' use of the Bozeman Trail through his tribe's lands in Colorado and Montana. The trail was later abandoned because of his efforts.

1876 – General George Custer and the U.S. Seventh Cavalry is wiped out at the Battle of the Little Bighorn by Native Americans led by Sioux Chief Sitting Bull.

1890 – The massacre at Wounded Knee marks the end of the Indian wars. Over 200 Sioux men, women, and children were killed by cavalry troops as they were camped along the Wounded Knee Creek in South Dakota.

INDEX ⬥

FURTHER READING

America's Fascinating Indian Heritage: The First Americans, Their Customs, Art, History, and How They Lived. Pleasantville, NY: Reader's Digest Publishing, 1996.

Indians of North America (series). Philadelphia: Chelsea House Publishers.

Joseph, Alvin M. Jr. *500 Nations: An Illustrated History of North American Indians.* New York: Knopf, 1994.

North American Indians of Achievement (series) Philadelphia: Chelsea House Publishers.

Pierce, Trudy Griffin. *Native Americans: Enduring Cultures and Traditions.* New York: Metro Books, 1996

Sherman, Joseph. *The First Americans: Spirit of the Land and the People.* New York: Smithmark Publishers, 1996.